JAMES STEVENSON

I HAD A LOT OF WISHES

STAR LIGHT
STAR BRIGHT
FIRST STAR I SEE TONIGHT
I WISH I MAY
I WISH I MIGHT
GET THE WISH
I WISH TONIGHT

GREENWILLOW BOOKS, NEW YORK

For Luca

Watercolor paintings were used
for the full-color art.
The text type is Bookman.

Printed in Singapore by KHL
Printing Co. Pte. Ltd.

First Edition
10 9 8 7 6 5 4 3 2 1

Library of Congress
Cataloging-in-Publication Data

Stevenson, James (date)
I had a lot of wishes / by James Stevenson.
    p.   cm.
ISBN 0-688-13705-9 (trade).
ISBN 0-688-13706-7 (lib. bdg.)
1. Stevenson, James (date)—Childhood
and youth—Juvenile literature.
2. Authors, American—20th century—
Biography—Juvenile literature.
3. Illustrators—United States—
Biography—Juvenile literature.
4. Wishes—Juvenile literature.
[1. Stevenson, James (date).
2. Authors, American.   3. Illustrators.]
I. Title.   PS3569.T4557Z4765   1995
813'.54—dc20   [B]   94-33420
CIP   AC

When I was young,
I had a lot of wishes.

All kinds of wishes.

WISHES THAT
SOMETHING WOULD
HAPPEN

WISHES THAT
SOMETHING
WOULD NOT
HAPPEN

WISHES THAT
WHAT WAS
HAPPENING
WOULD STOP

WISHES I COULD
GET SOMETHING
I DIDN'T HAVE

OR MAYBE
BORROW IT
FOR A WHILE

My wishes piled up.
Some were big.

I WISHED I HAD A REALLY FAST MOTORCYCLE AND WAS OLD ENOUGH TO RIDE IT.

I WISHED I HAD A LOT OF BROTHERS AND SISTERS SO WE COULD HAVE FUN ALL THE TIME.

Some were little.

WHEN AUNT MARJORIE BROUGHT A BOX OF CANDY AND I WAS ALLOWED ONLY ONE, I WISHED I'D GET THE KIND I LIKED.

(THE CHANCES WERE 50-50.)

UH... UH...

STOP DAWDLING AND JUST TAKE ONE

ANYBODY ELSE CARE FOR A CHOCOLATE?

OH, ICK!

Some were too-late wishes.

I WISHED I HADN'T GOT A SPLINTER (TOO LATE!)

OR SOMETHING IN MY EYE
(TOO LATE!)

OR POISON IVY
(TOO LATE!)

OR AN ICE-CREAM (TOO
HEADACHE LATE!)

OR THAT I'D CAUGHT THE BALL I WAS
SURE I WOULD CATCH --- TOO LATE!!

OOPS!

BUTTERFINGERS!
HOME RUN!

Most wishes were to make something happen.

PALACE

I WISHED MY MOTHER WOULD TAKE US TO
THE MOVIES OFTEN --- NOT JUST WHEN IT WAS
RAINING HARD AND THE MOVIE WAS 'WORTHWHILE'
AND THERE WAS NOTHING ELSE TO DO.

I wished my friends David
and Dorothy and Bill
were more fun.

I wished I could be a G-man, and capture gangsters
(or even *be* a gangster, if I didn't have to do
anything bad).

Some wishes were to make things stop.

I WISHED MR. RADICH
WOULDN'T BE MY HOMEROOM
TEACHER ANYMORE.

I WISHED THE COLTONS' DOG WOULD
STOP CHASING OUR DOG, JOCKO.

I WISHED
MY PARENTS
WOULD STOP
ARGUING
OVER NOTHING.

I wished they didn't give us what they
gave us at school for lunch.

BRUSSELS
SPROUTS

OLIVE LOAF

SALMON SALAD

CHOCOLATE
PUDDING

I wished my brother would stop
trying to scare me at night.

Some wishes were impossible,
but I wished them anyway.

Some were more like dreams.

There were someday-wishes, too.

MY FATHER WAS
AN ARCHITECT.
HE WORKED AT
A BIG DESK.

HE HAD A LOT OF GOOD STUFF ON HIS DESK.

RULERS

A
COMPASS

ERASERS

TRIANGLES

BRUSHES

THUMBTACKS

METAL
T-SQUARE

ROLLS OF
BLUE PAPER
AND YELLOW
TRACING PAPER

PENCILS

A TAPE MEASURE THAT WENT 25 FEET

(IT HAD A HANDLE SO YOU COULD REEL IT BACK IN.)

I wished I could try some of those things.
I asked my father if I could.
"Not right now," he said. "I'm busy."
"When can I?" I asked.
"Someday," he said. "When I'm not so busy."

That was a someday-wish.
I wished someday would hurry up.

Getting your wish wasn't easy.
There were four possible ways to do it.

One was by blowing out
all the candles
on your birthday cake
with one breath.
(The trouble with that
was you only got
one chance a year.)

The second way was to put
a tooth under your pillow.
(The trouble with that was you
had to have your tooth pulled out.)

The third way was to wish on
a star and recite a special poem.

Star wishes almost never worked.
Maybe it was the poem.
But I kept on trying, at least most nights.

The fourth way was the wishbone.

Whenever we had a chicken
for dinner, our mother saved
the wishbone.

She kept it for a week
until it was very dry.
(That gave us plenty
of time to think of wishes.)
Then my brother and I
each made a wish.

He held one leg
of the wishbone,
and I held the other.
Then we pulled . . .

SNAP!

Whoever had the biggest part got his wish—
my brother, usually.
It didn't seem fair.

He already had a football

and a Roosevelt button

and a plastic pickle pin
from the 1939 World's Fair.

If you wanted to get your wish,
it helped to be lucky.
One way to be lucky was to find
a four-leaf clover.

I looked and looked and looked, but I never found one.
I guess you had to be lucky.

When I didn't get my wish,
sometimes I'd say to myself,
"I wish I'd wished for an easier wish."

Sometimes I just wished I could stop wishing.

One year I wished I could go to camp.

Finally I got my wish!

I said good-bye to David and Dorothy and Bill

and Jocko.

I went on an overnight boat
from New York to Cape Cod
with other kids who were
going to camp.

I'd never been away from home. I couldn't sleep.

Camp Wampasokee wasn't exactly like the catalog.

IT HAD DARK TREES. IT LOOKED GLOOMY.

THERE WERE MOSQUITOES EVERYWHERE

AND FLIES AND WASPS AND TICKS AND YELLOW JACKETS.

THERE WERE HOT, SMELLY CABINS (WITH MOSQUITOES IN THEM).

THERE WERE BOSSY COUNSELORS,

AND A SPOOKY LAKE THAT MIGHT HAVE SNAPPING TURTLES.

A lot of the campers had gone to the camp before.
They didn't like new kids.

In arts and crafts they made you make things
you didn't want to make.

POUCH

BEADED BELT

I wished I hadn't got my wish.

MOM? CAN
I COME
HOME?
I DON'T
LIKE IT
HERE....
NO, I CAN'T
TALK
LOUDER....

My birthday came.
They gave me a cake.
Everybody sang "Happy Birthday."
I made a wish and blew out the candles.

I wished I could go home right away.

But slowly things got better.
We had contests and games.
I won the prize for swimming underwater.

We played softball against the counselors.
I got a hit.

Then, the last week, the whole camp went on a canoe trip.

We cooked hamburgers over a bonfire.
A counselor told us ghost stories.
It was great.

Then camp was over.
I said good-bye to my friends.

DANNY   LOU   ALVIN   PAUL

FRANK   TOM[1]   MARV   GREG

BILLY   DONALD   HENRY

TOM[2]   SAM

My parents and my brother picked me up
in our car, and we drove home
with the top down most of the way.
(It took two days because there were
no big highways then.)

When I got back, David and Dorothy and Bill
were more fun than I remembered.

I was glad to be home and to play
with Jocko again.

Now that I'm old,
I don't make too many wishes.

But a lot of the wishes I made
a long time ago are coming true.